SHIRLEY
TEMPLE BLACK

Gloria D. Miklowitz

ᵱᗖ **Dominie Press, Inc.**

Publisher: Raymond Yuen
Editor: John S. F. Graham
Designer: Greg DiGenti
Photo Credits: Bettmann/Corbis (cover and pages 7, 10, 14, 22, and 27) ; Hulton-Deutsch Collection/Corbis (Page 25)

Published by:

Dominie Press, Inc.
1949 Kellogg Avenue
Carlsbad, California 92008 USA

www.dominie.com

Paperback ISBN 0-7685-1222-0
Library Bound Edition ISBN 0-7685-1547-5
Printed in Singapore by PH Productions Pte Ltd
1 2 3 4 5 6 PH 04 03 02

Table of Contents

Chapter 1

The Little Princess

They called her "the little princess."
She appeared in more than 40 films and
was loved throughout the world. Shirley
Temple was born on April 23, 1928, in
Santa Monica, California. She was the
third child of George and Gertrude

Temple. George was a bank clerk and Gertrude was a homemaker.

"She ran on her toes as if she were dancing," Shirley's mother said. She often played the radio while she did housework. Shirley would follow her, acting and dancing to the music being played. She had a natural grace and seemed to really enjoy moving to music.

In 1931, when Shirley was barely 3, her mother enrolled her in the Meglin Dance Studio. It was a school that trained very young children for work in film and advertising. America was in the middle of the Great Depression. Many people were out of work. Although Shirley's father had a job, it was not easy to pay for lessons.

Shirley liked to please people and

Shirley Temple and her parents, George and Gertrude

loved the lessons. She listened and practiced hard. One day, when she was almost 4, a movie scout came to the school to choose children for movie parts. His name was Charles Lamont, a director for Educational Films Corporation.

Lamont frightened her, Shirley later wrote in her autobiography. So much so that she hid under a piano. The director stood around for a while, watching, then said, "I'll take the one under the piano."

Shirley and others from the school were given a screen test to see how they would photograph. Bright-eyed with curly hair, Shirley was also charming, and her personality and talent won her a contract.

Chapter 2

Stand Up and Cheer

After the film contract was signed, Shirley began to work in short films called, "Baby Burlesks," playing many parts. Only four years old, she earned $10 for each day she worked, a lot of money in the 1930s.

The films had young children act as grown-ups and made fun of adult movies. For instance, in *Kid in Africa*, Shirley played the role of Cradlebait, a missionary to Africa who gets captured by cannibals and saved by Diaperzan (Tarzan).

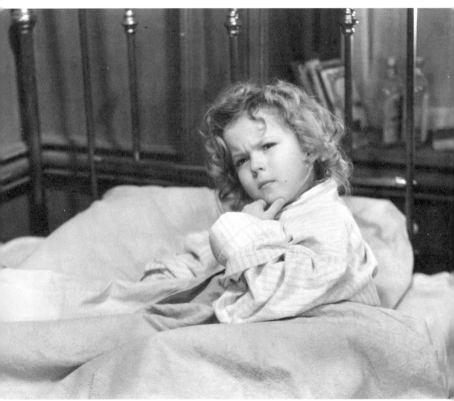

Shirley Temple in **Little Miss Marker**

In *Glad Rags to Riches*, Shirley played La Belle Diaper, a showgirl who sang "She's Only a Bird in a Gilded Cage."

And in *War Babies*, based on the adult film *What Price Glory*, Shirley imitated the actress who played the part of Charmaine and spoke most of her lines in French.

During 1932, she played in seven of these short films, earning about $300. But the series was canceled the next year. The child actors were getting older.

After that, she played small parts in a number of two-reel pictures. Then Fox Studios put out a call for children to sing and dance in the film *Scandals*. Her mother took her for an audition. There, she attracted interest from Leo Houck of Fox Studios. He introduced the Temple family to a songwriter named Jay Gorney, who was looking for a child to play a part in the musical *Stand Up and Cheer*. Shirley got the part.

Filmed in early 1934, Shirley did a song-and-dance sequence called "Baby, Take a Bow." Audiences and critics stood up and cheered.

"You're going to be the most loved little girl in the whole world," the writer Vincent Sheean said to her.

Chapter 3

The Ability to Radiate Happiness

In 1934, under contract to Fox studios at $150 per week, Shirley was on loan to Paramount Studios. There, she played in *Little Miss Marker*. In the movie, her father, a gambler, dies, and she is saved by the gambling house owner, who

Shirley Temple and Bill "Bojangles" Robinson in The Little Colonel

gives her a real home. During that year, she appeared in nine films!

In *Bright Eyes*, she sang "On the Good Ship Lollipop." It sold half a million copies in sheet music.

In *The Little Colonel*, a Civil War drama with music, Shirley danced up and down stairs with actor and tap dancer Bill "Bojangles" Robinson.

The film studios Shirley worked with were making enormous amounts of money. The theaters that showed her movies were also making a lot of money. Because of that success, her salary rose to $3,000 per week. More income came from Shirley Temple dolls, coloring books, dresses, and other things. Still, her mother only allowed Shirley $4.25 per week in allowance.

A bright child, Shirley's IQ was rated above the genius level. She learned difficult dance steps quickly "by ear" rather than watching the teacher's feet. In *Captain January*, she had to tap dance down a 45-foot staircase, saying a line at each step. She did it perfectly in one take.

The young actress had the ability to radiate happiness and hope when the world was deeply depressed. President Franklin D. Roosevelt said, "As long as our country has Shirley Temple, we will be all right."

Years later, Shirley said, "I class myself with [the famous dog] Rin Tin Tin. People in the Depression wanted something to cheer them up, and they fell in love with a dog and a little girl."

At the top of her fame, it seemed nothing could stop Shirley's success. But she was getting older.

Chapter 4

Sparkle

In 1935, a year after her amazing successes, Shirley Temple appeared in *Our Little Girl*, *Curly Top*, and *The Littlest Rebel*, in which she was again teamed with Bill Robinson in a film about the South. When *Curly Top* played at Radio City Music Hall in New York City, 5,000 people attended each showing. Long lines formed outside, waiting for the next show. She also received a special Academy Award for her film work the previous year.

The country went wild for Shirley. Shirley Temple dolls were selling at the rate of 1.5 million a year. She received 5,000 fan letters a week at home. Secretaries were hired to answer the mail. She was photographed as many as 20 times a day, more often than the President of the United States.

She loved what she was doing, and she worked hard. He mother, always at her side, acted as her hairdresser and coach. Each evening, she helped Shirley learn lines for the next day's filming. When filming was about to start, her mother would say, "Sparkle, Shirl!"

Shirley had an amazing ability to concentrate and learn quickly. A typical day found her in front of the cameras for three hours. A teacher worked with her on schoolwork for three more hours, usually between scenes. When time allowed, there were photo sessions and fittings for clothes. On weekends, she played with friends in the neighborhood.

In the next few years, Shirley performed very demanding song-and-dance routines and appeared in more films. But the films were much alike. One critic said, "For two years, Shirley has been doing the same thing. Give her more intelligent stories and better actors in the supporting roles."

From 1936 to 1938, she starred in

movies like *Heidi*, *Rebecca of Sunnybrook Farm*, and *The Little Princess*. She was ten years old and one of the most popular movie stars.

But by 1940, Shirley's films were not earning money like they used to. Now twelve, almost a teenager, she had been acting for nine years and had appeared in 44 films.

Chapter 5

Public Service

Shirley Temple's popularity began to decline in 1939 and 1940. Now that she was making fewer movies, she had time for other things. Her mother enrolled her in the Westlake School for Girls in Los Angeles so she could lead a more normal life.

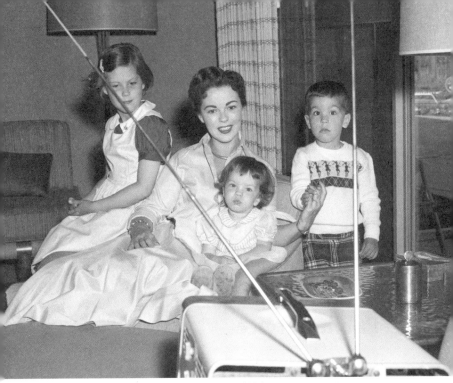

Shirley Temple and her children—Susan, 8; Lori, 2; and Charles, Jr., 4—watching television in their Atherton, California home

Around this time, the film studio Metro-Goldwyn-Mayer wanted her to star in *The Wizard of Oz*. But her contract with Fox Studios wouldn't allow her to work for another studio, and the president of Fox wouldn't let her go. Judy Garland starred in the movie instead.

Then, in 1940, Shirley's movie *The Blue Bird* did not make a profit. It was the last movie she would make with Fox Studios. Her old contract over, Metro-Goldwyn-Mayer signed her at $100,000 a year and allowed her to work in radio as well as films.

As World War II started, Shirley became a teenager. She could no longer star in the children's roles she once did.

In 1944, she appeared in *Since You Went Away*, a war film. Soldiers wrote asking for her photo and considered her their kid sister. A year later, after having starred in *Kiss and Tell*, she had to kiss some soldiers in a charity-kissing booth as a publicity stunt.

Shirley graduated from Westlake in 1945 at the age of 17, and married

Sergeant John Agar. In 1948, she had a daughter, Susan. She appeared in two well-received movies, *The Bachelor and the Bobby Soxer* and *Fort Apache*, in which she starred with her husband, John.

But the marriage ended in 1949, and she stopped appearing in movies. Divorced and the mother of a little girl, she decided to take the first real vacation of her life. She and Susan went to Hawaii. She had been to Hawaii before, but always with studio people, so she couldn't really relax.

Her movie career was over, but she was having the time of her life. In Hawaii, she met San Francisco business executive and naval officer Charles Black and fell in love. They married in 1950, and she had two more children in the following years, Charles, Jr. and Lori.

Shirley Temple Black and her husband, Charles Black

When the Korean War broke out, Charles was assigned to Washington D.C. There, Shirley met many people in high government positions and became interested in politics. About that time, she also learned that most of the money she earned as a child had been poorly invested by her father.

Returning to California in 1954, she received movie and television offers. But her interest now turned to public service. In 1967, she ran for Congress in California. She lost the election, but she didn't lose her interest in serving her country.

Shirley Temple Black has served the United States under four presidents, having been ambassador to Ghana and Czechoslovakia (and later, the Czech Republic), representative to the United Nations, and the United States chief of protocol.

In 1983, Shirley helped start The American Academy of Diplomacy, which helps to improve the United States' relations with other countries. Although retired now, she has devoted her life to the cause of international relations. Most people know Shirley for her work in the movies, but that was just a small part of what she did for her country.

Shirley Temple Black is sworn in as a delegate to the United Nations

Glossary

Academy - a type of private high school.

Ambassador - someone who represents a nation to other nations or to a global organization.

Audition - when an actor or actress tries out for a role in a movie or play.

Autobiography - a book written by someone who tells about his or her life. A *biography* is a book written about someone, but is written by someone else.

Bachelor - a man who isn't married.

Bobby Soxer - a term in the 1940s and 1950s for a girl who is not a child, but isn't yet a woman.

Colonel - an officer's rank in the army between Major and General.

Contract - a legal agreement between two people or groups that says what both must do for each other.

Czechoslovakia - a small country that used to be in Eastern Europe. In 1989, it split up into two different countries: Slovakia and the Czech Republic.

Diplomacy - how countries treat each other.

Director - a person who organizes the action of making a movie.

Enrolled - when someone is going to school.

Executive - a high-level businessperson.

Great Depression - a time in the 1930s when the U.S. economy was so bad that hundreds of thousands of people lost their jobs. After some bad investments, many banks failed and many more businesses and farms had to close down.

IQ - one measure of how intelligent someone is. It stands for Intelligence Quotient, and represents a score someone gets on an IQ test.

Missionary - a religious person who travels to different places to try and convert people to a religion.

Personality - the way someone acts around other people.

Protocol - the way to treat people from other countries.

Radiate - to shine; to project something.

Studio - a room where creative productions, like movies, dances, and plays, are performed and rehearsed. Film studios can also be a collection of these rooms that belong to one company.

Salary - a regular payment given to an employee of a company or organization.

Sequence - more than one of something that happens one at a time.

Sergeant - a rank in the army between Corporal and Lieutenant.

Showgirl - a woman who dances in theater shows and musicals.

Starred - featured in a movie or theater production.

Two-Reel Movie - a short movie. A reel of film holds about 22 minutes, so a movie that has two reels lasts for about 44 minutes. Most movies last between one-and-a-half hours and two-hours, which can be up to six reels.